If Found, Please Return To:

Name:

_____

Phone Number:

_____

Property 1

Address	
Date of Purchase	
Purchase Price	
Appraised Value	

Type of Property:

☐ Single Family Dwelling

☐ Duplex

☐ Apartment

☐ Condo

☐ Other

Property Details:

_____ Bedrooms

_____ Bathrooms

Other Details: _____

_____

_____

Financing Information

Mortgage Company	
	Name:
	Address:
	Loan Officer:
	Phone:
	Email:
Loan Number	
Date Opened	
Amount Financed	
Interest Rate	
Number of Payments	
Monthly Payment	
Due Date	

Other Financing Notes:

Insurance Information
Liability

Insurance Company	
	Name: _____ Address: _____
	Agent: _____ Phone: _____ Email: _____
Policy Number	
Coverage	
Annual Premium	
Renewal Date	

Other Liability Insurance Information: _____

_____

_____

_____

_____

_____

_____

Insurance Information
Property

Insurance Company	Name: _____
	Address:
	_____
	Agent: _____
	Phone: _____
	Email: _____
Policy Number	
Coverage	
Annual Premium	
Renewal Date	

Other Property Insurance Information: _____

_____

_____

_____

_____

_____

_____

Maintenance Log

Date	Damage	Cause	Cost	Notes

Maintenance Log

Date	Damage	Cause	Cost	Notes

Maintenance Log

Date	Damage	Cause	Cost	Notes

Maintenance Log

Date	Damage	Cause	Cost	Notes

Maintenance Log

Date	Damage	Cause	Cost	Notes

Prospective Tenant Interview

Full Name: _____

Current Address: _____

_____

Phone Number: _____

Email: _____

Date of Birth: _____ SS#: _____

[ ] Criminal History Check Done   [ ] Credit History Check Done

Current Employer: _____

Supervisor Name: _____

Supervisor Phone Number: _____

Employed Since: _____ Monthly Net Pay: _____

Unit Size Requested: _____ Date Needed: _____

Individuals Authorized To Reside Unit: _____

Pets Authorized To Reside In Unit: [ ] Yes [ ] No

Prospective Tenant Interview Continued

Personal References

Name	Number	Notes

Prior Rental References

Name	Number	Notes

Other Interview Notes: _____

_____

_____

_____

Prospective Tenant Interview

Full Name: _____

Current Address: _____

_____

Phone Number: _____

Email: _____

Date of Birth: _____ SS#: _____

[ ] Criminal History
    Check Done

[ ] Credit History
    Check Done

Current Employer: _____

Supervisor Name: _____

Supervisor Phone Number: _____

Employed Since: _____ Monthly Net Pay: _____

Unit Size Requested: _____ Date Needed: _____

Individuals Authorized To Reside Unit: _____

Pets Authorized To Reside In Unit: [ ] Yes   [ ] No

Prospective Tenant Interview Continued

Personal References

Name	Number	Notes

Prior Rental References

Name	Number	Notes

Other Interview Notes: _____

_____

_____

_____

Prospective Tenant Interview

Full Name: _____

Current Address: _____

_____

Phone Number: _____

Email: _____

Date of Birth: _____ SS#: _____

☐ Criminal History
Check Done

☐ Credit History
Check Done

Current Employer: _____

Supervisor Name: _____

Supervisor Phone Number: _____

Employed Since: _____ Monthly Net Pay: _____

Unit Size Requested: _____ Date Needed: _____

Individuals Authorized To Reside Unit: _____

Pets Authorized To Reside In Unit: ☐ Yes ☐ No

Prospective Tenant Interview Continued

Personal References

Name	Number	Notes

Prior Rental References

Name	Number	Notes

Other Interview Notes: _____

_____

_____

_____

Prospective Tenant Interview

Full Name: _____

Current Address: _____

_____

Phone Number: _____

Email: _____

Date of Birth: _____ SS#: _____

☐ Criminal History
  Check Done

☐ Credit History
  Check Done

Current Employer: _____

Supervisor Name: _____

Supervisor Phone Number: _____

Employed Since: _____ Monthly Net Pay: _____

Unit Size Requested: _____ Date Needed: _____

Individuals Authorized To Reside Unit: _____

Pets Authorized To Reside In Unit: ☐ Yes ☐ No

Prospective Tenant Interview Continued

Personal References

Name	Number	Notes

Prior Rental References

Name	Number	Notes

Other Interview Notes: _____

_____

_____

_____

Prospective Tenant Interview

Full Name: _____

Current Address: _____

_____

Phone Number: _____

Email: _____

Date of Birth: _____ SS#: _____

☐ Criminal History
Check Done

☐ Credit History
Check Done

Current Employer: _____

Supervisor Name: _____

Supervisor Phone Number: _____

Employed Since: _____ Monthly Net Pay: _____

Unit Size Requested: _____ Date Needed: _____

Individuals Authorized To Reside Unit: _____

Pets Authorized To Reside In Unit: ☐ Yes ☐ No

Prospective Tenant Interview Continued

Personal References

Name	Number	Notes

Prior Rental References

Name	Number	Notes

Other Interview Notes: _____

_____

_____

_____

Prospective Tenant Interview

Full Name: _____

Current Address: _____

_____

Phone Number: _____

Email: _____

Date of Birth: _____   SS#: _____

☐ Criminal History Check Done   ☐ Credit History Check Done

Current Employer: _____

Supervisor Name: _____

Supervisor Phone Number: _____

Employed Since: _____   Monthly Net Pay: _____

Unit Size Requested: _____   Date Needed: _____

Individuals Authorized To Reside Unit: _____

Pets Authorized To Reside In Unit: ☐ Yes   ☐ No

Prospective Tenant Interview Continued

Personal References

Name	Number	Notes

Prior Rental References

Name	Number	Notes

Other Interview Notes: _____

_____

_____

_____

Income Log

Date	Amount	From	Cash/Check	Notes

Income Log

Date	Amount	From	Cash/Check	Notes

Income Log

Date	Amount	From	Cash/Check	Notes

Income Log

Date	Amount	From	Cash/Check	Notes

Income Log

Date	Amount	From	Cash/Check	Notes

Expense Log

Date	Check No.	Amount	To	For

Expense Log

Date	Check No.	Amount	To	For

Expense Log

Date	Check No.	Amount	To	For

Expense Log

Date	Check No.	Amount	To	For

Expense Log

Date	Check No.	Amount	To	For

Property Overview

Year:	Total Income	Total Expenses	Net Profit/Loss
January			
February			
March			
April			
May			
June			
July			
August			
September			
October			
November			
December			
Total			

Year End Review: _____

_____

_____

_____

_____

_____

Property Overview

Year:	Total Income	Total Expenses	Net Profit/Loss
January			
February			
March			
April			
May			
June			
July			
August			
September			
October			
November			
December			
Total			

Year End Review: _____

_____

_____

_____

_____

Property Overview

Year:	Total Income	Total Expenses	Net Profit/Loss
January			
February			
March			
April			
May			
June			
July			
August			
September			
October			
November			
December			
Total			

Year End Review: _____

_____

_____

_____

_____

_____

Property Overview

Year:	Total Income	Total Expenses	Net Profit/Loss
January			
February			
March			
April			
May			
June			
July			
August			
September			
October			
November			
December			
Total			

Year End Review: _____

_____

_____

_____

_____

_____

Property Overview

Year:	Total Income	Total Expenses	Net Profit/Loss
January			
February			
March			
April			
May			
June			
July			
August			
September			
October			
November			
December			
Total			

Year End Review: _____

_____

_____

_____

_____

_____

Property 2

Address	
Date of Purchase	
Purchase Price	
Appraised Value	

Type of Property:

☐ Single Family Dwelling

☐ Duplex

☐ Apartment

☐ Condo

☐ Other

Property Details:

_____ Bedrooms

_____ Bathrooms

Other Details: _____

_____

_____

Financing Information

Mortgage Company	
	Name:
	Address:
	Loan Officer:
	Phone:
	Email:
Loan Number	
Date Opened	
Amount Financed	
Interest Rate	
Number of Payments	
Monthly Payment	
Due Date	

Other Financing Notes:

Insurance Information
Liability

Insurance Company	Name: _____
	Address: _____
	Agent: _____
	Phone: _____
	Email: _____
Policy Number	
Coverage	
Annual Premium	
Renewal Date	

Other Liability Insurance Information: _____

_____

_____

_____

_____

_____

Insurance Information
Property

Insurance Company	Name: _____
	Address: _____
	_____
	Agent: _____
	Phone: _____
	Email: _____
Policy Number	
Coverage	
Annual Premium	
Renewal Date	

Other Property Insurance Information: _____

_____

_____

_____

_____

_____

_____

Maintenance Log

Date	Damage	Cause	Cost	Notes

Maintenance Log

Date	Damage	Cause	Cost	Notes

Maintenance Log

Date	Damage	Cause	Cost	Notes

Maintenance Log

Date	Damage	Cause	Cost	Notes

Maintenance Log

Date	Damage	Cause	Cost	Notes

Prospective Tenant Interview

Full Name: _____

Current Address: _____

_____

Phone Number: _____

Email: _____

Date of Birth: _____ SS#: _____

[ ] Criminal History Check Done   [ ] Credit History Check Done

Current Employer: _____

Supervisor Name: _____

Supervisor Phone Number: _____

Employed Since: _____ Monthly Net Pay: _____

Unit Size Requested: _____ Date Needed: _____

Individuals Authorized To Reside Unit: _____

Pets Authorized To Reside In Unit: [ ] Yes [ ] No

Prospective Tenant Interview Continued

Personal References

Name	Number	Notes

Prior Rental References

Name	Number	Notes

Other Interview Notes: _____

_____

_____

_____

Prospective Tenant Interview

Full Name: _____

Current Address: _____

_____

Phone Number: _____

Email: _____

Date of Birth: _____ SS#: _____

☐ Criminal History
Check Done

☐ Credit History
Check Done

Current Employer: _____

Supervisor Name: _____

Supervisor Phone Number: _____

Employed Since: _____ Monthly Net Pay: _____

Unit Size Requested: _____ Date Needed: _____

Individuals Authorized To Reside Unit: _____

Pets Authorized To Reside In Unit: ☐ Yes ☐ No

Prospective Tenant Interview Continued

Personal References

Name	Number	Notes

Prior Rental References

Name	Number	Notes

Other Interview Notes: _____

_____

_____

_____

Prospective Tenant Interview

Full Name: _____

Current Address: _____

_____

Phone Number: _____

Email: _____

Date of Birth: _____ SS#: _____

☐ Criminal History Check Done   ☐ Credit History Check Done

Current Employer: _____

Supervisor Name: _____

Supervisor Phone Number: _____

Employed Since: _____ Monthly Net Pay: _____

Unit Size Requested: _____ Date Needed: _____

Individuals Authorized To Reside Unit: _____

_____

Pets Authorized To Reside In Unit: ☐ Yes ☐ No

_____

Prospective Tenant Interview Continued

Personal References

Name	Number	Notes

Prior Rental References

Name	Number	Notes

Other Interview Notes: _____

_____

_____

_____

Prospective Tenant Interview

Full Name: _____

Current Address: _____

_____

Phone Number: _____

Email: _____

Date of Birth: _____ SS#: _____

☐ Criminal History Check Done   ☐ Credit History Check Done

Current Employer: _____

Supervisor Name: _____

Supervisor Phone Number: _____

Employed Since: _____ Monthly Net Pay: _____

Unit Size Requested: _____ Date Needed: _____

Individuals Authorized To Reside Unit: _____

_____

Pets Authorized To Reside In Unit: ☐ Yes   ☐ No

Prospective Tenant Interview Continued

Personal References

Name	Number	Notes

Prior Rental References

Name	Number	Notes

Other Interview Notes: _____

_____

_____

_____

Prospective Tenant Interview

Full Name: _____

Current Address: _____

_____

Phone Number: _____

Email: _____

Date of Birth: _____ SS#: _____

☐ Criminal History Check Done   ☐ Credit History Check Done

Current Employer: _____

Supervisor Name: _____

Supervisor Phone Number: _____

Employed Since: _____ Monthly Net Pay: _____

Unit Size Requested: _____ Date Needed: _____

Individuals Authorized To Reside Unit: _____

Pets Authorized To Reside In Unit: ☐ Yes ☐ No

Prospective Tenant Interview Continued

Personal References

Name	Number	Notes

Prior Rental References

Name	Number	Notes

Other Interview Notes: _____

_____

_____

_____

Prospective Tenant Interview

Full Name: _____

Current Address: _____
_____

Phone Number: _____

Email: _____

Date of Birth: _____ SS#: _____

[ ] Criminal History
Check Done

[ ] Credit History
Check Done

Current Employer: _____

Supervisor Name: _____

Supervisor Phone Number: _____

Employed Since: _____ Monthly Net Pay: _____

Unit Size Requested: _____ Date Needed: _____

Individuals Authorized To Reside Unit: _____

Pets Authorized To Reside In Unit: [ ] Yes [ ] No

Prospective Tenant Interview Continued

Personal References

Name	Number	Notes

Prior Rental References

Name	Number	Notes

Other Interview Notes: _____

_____

_____

_____

Income Log

Date	Amount	From	Cash/Check	Notes

Income Log

Date	Amount	From	Cash/Check	Notes

Income Log

Date	Amount	From	Cash/Check	Notes

Income Log

Date	Amount	From	Cash/Check	Notes

Income Log

Date	Amount	From	Cash/Check	Notes

Expense Log

Date	Check No.	Amount	To	For

Expense Log

Date	Check No.	Amount	To	For

Expense Log

Date	Check No.	Amount	To	For

Expense Log

Date	Check No.	Amount	To	For

Expense Log

Date	Check No.	Amount	To	For

Property Overview

Year:	Total Income	Total Expenses	Net Profit/Loss
January			
February			
March			
April			
May			
June			
July			
August			
September			
October			
November			
December			
Total			

Year End Review: _____

_____

_____

_____

_____

_____

Property Overview

Year:	Total Income	Total Expenses	Net Profit/Loss
January			
February			
March			
April			
May			
June			
July			
August			
September			
October			
November			
December			
Total			

Year End Review: _____

_____

_____

_____

_____

Property Overview

Year:	Total Income	Total Expenses	Net Profit/Loss
January			
February			
March			
April			
May			
June			
July			
August			
September			
October			
November			
December			
Total			

Year End Review: _____

_____

_____

_____

_____

_____

Property Overview

Year:	Total Income	Total Expenses	Net Profit/Loss
January			
February			
March			
April			
May			
June			
July			
August			
September			
October			
November			
December			
Total			

Year End Review: _____

_____

_____

_____

_____

_____

Property Overview

Year:	Total Income	Total Expenses	Net Profit/Loss
January			
February			
March			
April			
May			
June			
July			
August			
September			
October			
November			
December			
Total			

Year End Review: _____

_____

_____

_____

_____

_____

Property 3

Address	
Date of Purchase	
Purchase Price	
Appraised Value	

Type of Property:

☐ Single Family Dwelling

☐ Duplex

☐ Apartment

☐ Condo

☐ Other

Property Details:

_____ Bedrooms

_____ Bathrooms

Other Details: _____

_____

_____

Financing Information

Mortgage Company	
	Name:
	Address:
	Loan Officer:
	Phone:
	Email:
Loan Number	
Date Opened	
Amount Financed	
Interest Rate	
Number of Payments	
Monthly Payment	
Due Date	

Other Financing Notes:

Insurance Information
Liability

Insurance Company		
	Name: _____	
	Address: _____	
	Agent: _____	
	Phone: _____	
	Email: _____	
Policy Number		
Coverage		
Annual Premium		
Renewal Date		

Other Liability Insurance Information: _____

_____

_____

_____

_____

_____

_____

Insurance Information
Property

Insurance Company	Name: _____
	Address: _____
	_____
	Agent: _____
	Phone: _____
	Email: _____
Policy Number	
Coverage	
Annual Premium	
Renewal Date	

Other Property Insurance Information: _____

_____

_____

_____

_____

_____

_____

Maintenance Log

Date	Damage	Cause	Cost	Notes

Maintenance Log

Date	Damage	Cause	Cost	Notes

Maintenance Log

Date	Damage	Cause	Cost	Notes

Maintenance Log

Date	Damage	Cause	Cost	Notes

Maintenance Log

Date	Damage	Cause	Cost	Notes

Prospective Tenant Interview

Full Name: _____

Current Address: _____

_____

Phone Number: _____

Email: _____

Date of Birth: _____ SS#: _____

☐ Criminal History
Check Done

☐ Credit History
Check Done

Current Employer: _____

Supervisor Name: _____

Supervisor Phone Number: _____

Employed Since: _____ Monthly Net Pay: _____

Unit Size Requested: _____ Date Needed: _____

Individuals Authorized To Reside Unit: _____

_____

Pets Authorized To Reside In Unit: ☐ Yes ☐ No

Prospective Tenant Interview Continued

Personal References

Name	Number	Notes

Prior Rental References

Name	Number	Notes

Other Interview Notes: _____

_____

_____

_____

Prospective Tenant Interview

Full Name: _____

Current Address: _____

_____

Phone Number: _____

Email: _____

Date of Birth: _____ SS#: _____

☐ Criminal History Check Done   ☐ Credit History Check Done

Current Employer: _____

Supervisor Name: _____

Supervisor Phone Number: _____

Employed Since: _____ Monthly Net Pay: _____

Unit Size Requested: _____ Date Needed: _____

Individuals Authorized To Reside Unit: _____

Pets Authorized To Reside In Unit: ☐ Yes   ☐ No

Prospective Tenant Interview Continued

Personal References

Name	Number	Notes

Prior Rental References

Name	Number	Notes

Other Interview Notes: _____

_____

_____

_____

Prospective Tenant Interview

Full Name: _____

Current Address: _____

_____

Phone Number: _____

Email: _____

Date of Birth: _____ SS#: _____

☐ Criminal History
Check Done

☐ Credit History
Check Done

Current Employer: _____

Supervisor Name: _____

Supervisor Phone Number: _____

Employed Since: _____ Monthly Net Pay: _____

Unit Size Requested: _____ Date Needed: _____

Individuals Authorized To Reside Unit: _____

Pets Authorized To Reside In Unit: ☐ Yes ☐ No

Prospective Tenant Interview Continued

Personal References

Name	Number	Notes

Prior Rental References

Name	Number	Notes

Other Interview Notes: _____

_____

_____

_____

Prospective Tenant Interview

Full Name: _____

Current Address: _____

_____

Phone Number: _____

Email: _____

Date of Birth: _____ SS#: _____

☐ Criminal History Check Done   ☐ Credit History Check Done

Current Employer: _____

Supervisor Name: _____

Supervisor Phone Number: _____

Employed Since: _____ Monthly Net Pay: _____

Unit Size Requested: _____ Date Needed: _____

Individuals Authorized To Reside Unit: _____

Pets Authorized To Reside In Unit: ☐ Yes ☐ No

Prospective Tenant Interview Continued

Personal References

Name	Number	Notes

Prior Rental References

Name	Number	Notes

Other Interview Notes: _____

_____

_____

_____

Prospective Tenant Interview

Full Name: _____

Current Address: _____

_____

Phone Number: _____

Email: _____

Date of Birth: _____ SS#: _____

[ ] Criminal History
     Check Done

[ ] Credit History
     Check Done

Current Employer: _____

Supervisor Name: _____

Supervisor Phone Number: _____

Employed Since: _____ Monthly Net Pay: _____

Unit Size Requested: _____ Date Needed: _____

Individuals Authorized To Reside Unit: _____

Pets Authorized To Reside In Unit: [ ] Yes   [ ] No

Prospective Tenant Interview Continued

Personal References

Name	Number	Notes

Prior Rental References

Name	Number	Notes

Other Interview Notes: _____

_____

_____

_____

Prospective Tenant Interview

Full Name: _____

Current Address: _____

_____

Phone Number: _____

Email: _____

Date of Birth: _____ SS#: _____

☐ Criminal History Check Done ☐ Credit History Check Done

Current Employer: _____

Supervisor Name: _____

Supervisor Phone Number: _____

Employed Since: _____ Monthly Net Pay: _____

Unit Size Requested: _____ Date Needed: _____

Individuals Authorized To Reside Unit: _____

Pets Authorized To Reside In Unit: ☐ Yes ☐ No

Prospective Tenant Interview Continued

Personal References

Name	Number	Notes

Prior Rental References

Name	Number	Notes

Other Interview Notes: _____

_____

_____

_____

Income Log

Date	Amount	From	Cash/Check	Notes

Income Log

Date	Amount	From	Cash/Check	Notes

Income Log

Date	Amount	From	Cash/Check	Notes

Income Log

Date	Amount	From	Cash/Check	Notes

Income Log

Date	Amount	From	Cash/Check	Notes

Expense Log

Date	Check No.	Amount	To	For

Expense Log

Date	Check No.	Amount	To	For

Expense Log

Date	Check No.	Amount	To	For

Expense Log

Date	Check No.	Amount	To	For

Expense Log

Date	Check No.	Amount	To	For

Property Overview

Year:	Total Income	Total Expenses	Net Profit/Loss
January			
February			
March			
April			
May			
June			
July			
August			
September			
October			
November			
December			
Total			

Year End Review: _____

_____

_____

_____

_____

_____

Property Overview

Year:	Total Income	Total Expenses	Net Profit/Loss
January			
February			
March			
April			
May			
June			
July			
August			
September			
October			
November			
December			
Total			

Year End Review: _____

_____

_____

_____

_____

Property Overview

Year:	Total Income	Total Expenses	Net Profit/Loss
January			
February			
March			
April			
May			
June			
July			
August			
September			
October			
November			
December			
Total			

Year End Review: _____

_____

_____

_____

_____

_____

Property Overview

Year:	Total Income	Total Expenses	Net Profit/Loss
January			
February			
March			
April			
May			
June			
July			
August			
September			
October			
November			
December			
Total			

Year End Review: _____

_____

_____

_____

_____

_____

Property Overview

Year:	Total Income	Total Expenses	Net Profit/Loss
January			
February			
March			
April			
May			
June			
July			
August			
September			
October			
November			
December			
Total			

Year End Review: _____

_____

_____

_____

_____

_____

Notes

Notes

Notes

Notes

Notes

Notes

Notes

Notes

Notes

Notes

Notes

www.ingramcontent.com/pod-product-compliance
Lightning Source LLC
Chambersburg PA
CBHW072145170526
45158CB00004BA/1516